The Path to Extraordinary

Your Blueprint for Personal Growth

Table of Contents

Personal development is a major time-saver. The better you become, the less time it takes you to achieve your goals.

Chapter 1. Introduction

Delve into the transformative pages of our groundbreaking Special Report: "The Path to Extraordinary: Your Blueprint for Personal Growth". Not a technical manual, but instead, a radiant beacon guiding you towards the highest versions of yourself. Each page, each word, is a thoughtfully designed step leading to a voyage of self-discovery and growth. In our increasingly fast-paced, technology-driven world, it has never been more important to invest in yourself and this, dear reader, is your golden buyer's opportunity. This report, short of being an Aladdin's Lamp, will inspire, invigorate, and illuminate your path to reach the zenith of your unlimited potential. Discover with us the life-altering power of consistent growth and the breathtaking view from the extraordinary summit of personal achievement. Let's embark on this exciting journey together!

Chapter 2. Unleashing Your Potential

In the captivating universe of human potential, the most profound paradoxes reside. Every one of us is gifted with an incredible breadth and depth of untapped abilities, often uncharted and unidentified, waiting to be explored and unleashed. As we delve into the intricacies of human potential, we are essentially embarking on a voyage of self-discovery, of acknowledging our dormant strength, our buried capacity for brilliance. This chapter aims to commence that expedition, thus, broadening the horizons of our self-identity, self-efficacy, and self-realization.

2.1. The Concept of Human Potential

Recognizing the idea behind human potential is foundational to one's journey towards self-awakening and self-growth. Our potential encompasses our ability to transform abilities and dreams into reality, the dynamic vehicle by which we move from the dormant to the kinetic. It is the grand tapestry of skills, talents, and capacities that we have within us. The human agency is a fertile field waiting for the seeds of potential to be planted, nurtured, and cultivated.

Traditionally, society, cultures, families, and education systems around the world have often focused on identifying and correcting deficiencies in individuals, what one might term a 'deficit orientation'. However, particularly in the area of positive psychology, there has been a shift towards recognizing and harnessing potential, a more 'asset orientation'. This ideological transformation forms the foundation of our exploration into the concept of 'unleashing your potential'.

2.2. Identifying Your Inner Potential

Defining our potential is an enigmatic procedure, but it commences with the process of introspection. Our potential is deeply woven into the fabric of our identity and experiences, as well as our dreams and passions. Potential takes many forms, whether that be intellectual, creative, emotional, or physical. Therefore, identifying your individual potential requires you to delve deeper into what excites you, drives you, challenges you, and ultimately, fulfils you.

Start by understanding your passions and pursuits. What fires your curiosity? When do you feel the most driven and alive? Look for the spaces where your skills and interests intersect. It is here that you will often find the clearest indications of your potential. Our potential is not always apparent, but it resides in the distinctive confluence of our abilities and our passions.

2.3. Overcoming the Fear Barrier

Fear is often the one colossal hurdle that hinders the unfolding of our potential. Fear of failure, fear of judgement, fear of the unknown, these all are potent inhibitors stalling the process of exploring one's potential.

To overcome this fear barrier, consider adopting a growth mentality: view every setback, every disappointment, every failure, not as an insurmountable barrier, but as an opportunity for learning and growth. Remember that every master was once a beginner and every winner was once a contender that refused to give up.

Reframe your lenses to view failure not as an antithesis of success but as its inherent and indispensable component. For it's often said that "failure is the condiment that gives success its flavor."

2.4. Nurturing Your Potential

Once the potential is identified, the true journey begins. To fully utilize your potential, it needs to be nurtured, fostered, and allowed to grow, much like a sapling.

This process of nurturing happens over time and involves incrementally improving your skills, expanding your horizons, and stepping out of your comfort zone. Engage in activities aligned with your passions, seek opportunities for personal and professional growth, and, most importantly, be consistent with your efforts.

Remember, the journey to tapping your full potential is not necessarily a huge leap but a series of small, manageable steps leading towards self-improvement and self-actualization.

In conclusion, the journey of unleashing potential is a transition from the embryonic state of self-perception to the enlightened state of self-actualization. It is a path beset with challenges, yes, but it is also a path laden with fulfilling rewards. As you journey forward, find courage in the idea that the potential within you is immense, constant, awaiting your claim. Be patient, be intentional, and most importantly, remember that within you lies a limitless scope for greatness. This chapter was a starting point to help you recognize, and ultimately unleash, your extraordinary potential.

Chapter 3. Recognizing Your Strengths

As we sail in the astonishing waters of self-discovery and personal growth, it's essential to know and understand our strengths. Our individual strengths are intrinsic skills, talents, and abilities that significantly influence how we see the world and handle challenges. By recognizing and embracing these, we establish a foundation upon which to build achievements, persist through difficulties, and create a fulfilling, beneficial life. Acknowledging your strengths needs sincerity, introspection, and continuous contemplation. In perspective, it opens doors to potential, opportunity, understanding, and profound self-realization.

3.1. Identification and Introspection

Our journey's first step in recognizing strengths involves identifying what they are. Yet, many of us find it easier to pinpoint our weaknesses than strengths. Recognition begins within; by introspective analysis, frequent reflection, and gaining insight from past experiences. Identify the activities which come naturally to you, where you excel without much strain, and where you enjoy your 'flow' state.

Tune into your emotions during these activities. What empowers or ignites your passion? When do you feel most alive, most 'you'? Reflect on compliments and positive feedback you've received - these are external clues illuminated by those who witness you at your best. There's an undoubted strength where passion, skill, and recognition intersect.

3.2. Strengths and Values: Unveiling the Connection

Our values, those enduring beliefs that shape our worldview and guide our decisions, often align with our strengths. A valuable method for uncovering your strengths is to clarify what you value - and understanding how your actions testify to these values.

Consider an imaginary scenario: you value honesty and have a unique ability to communicate truthfully and candidly without offending others. This nuanced skill is a strength—your innate talent for diplomatic honesty.

3.3. Strengths Application: The Power of Leveraging

Once mapped, strengths can be leveraged as powerful tools for personal and professional growth. Utilizing your strengths can lead to increased happiness, reduced stress, and improved performance. Reflect on the opportunities for applying your unique abilities across assorted facets of your life. Seek instances wherein you can use a strength to overcome a challenge, thrive at your job, cultivate relationships, or merely to enjoy life to its fullest.

3.4. Challenges in Recognizing Your Strengths

While recognizing strengths may sound straightforward, it's not bereft of challenges - a significant one being the risk of overuse. It's critical to understand that strengths, when overused or inappropriately applied, can become weaknesses.

A person known for their determination and dedication could be seen as obstinate when refusing to reconsider a decision despite receiving contrasting information. Therefore, it's essential to cultivate an equilibrium in using our strengths, understanding when and how they can best serve us and others around us.

3.5. Enhancing Your Strengths: The Power of Practice

Merely recognizing your strengths isn't enough; honing them is equally crucial. This involves consistent practice and seeking new opportunities to apply your strengths. Undertake strategic learning focusing on these strengths – read books, take courses, find a mentor - saturate your mind with knowledge pertaining to your strengths. Dexterity and mastery can turn a strength into an invincible superpower.

3.6. The Role of Feedback

Finally, let's acknowledge the significant role feedback plays. While self-reflection is vital, sometimes, we could have blind spots preventing us from recognizing certain strengths. Here, a trusted mentor, coach, or peer can offer external perspective and help illuminate those strengths that we might unintentionally overlook or diminish.

In this exceptional journey of self-discovery, growth, and building extraordinary lives, recognizing our strengths is our compass, guiding us towards paths best suited for us. It's an ongoing, evolving process - a beautiful dance of self-awareness, conscious application, and continuous learning. See these strengths as personal assets, and apply them for maximum benefit. Over time, you'll witness an incredible transformation and growth burgeoning from the inside out, radiating outwards into the wider world.

Chapter 4. Overcoming Your Weaknesses

Overcoming weaknesses is undoubtedly a crucial component of personal growth. In this comprehensive write-up, we will carefully dissect this intricate subject matter, exploring the depths of its nuances and providing you with concrete strategies to conquer your weaknesses. To truly shatter the shackles of your limitations, it is vital not just to comprehend the issue at hand, but to get to the root of it. This chapter will guide you through the complex maze of understanding, acknowledging, and finally, overcoming your limitations.

4.1. Understanding Weaknesses

In delving deep into the realm of personal growth, it is vital that we grasp the concept of weaknesses in full measure. Humans, by design, aren't perfect; we each have our unique set of weaknesses that plague our everyday lives. These could range from performance-related issues like public speaking anxiety or procrastination, emotional vulnerabilities like a quick temper or excessive self-doubt, or could be knowledge gaps in professional or personal domains.

Understanding weaknesses, consequently, is the initial step towards overcoming them. A potent starting point in this journey is "self-awareness". Being genuinely aware of your foibles, your areas of struggle, gives you the power to deal with them. It involves introspection and reflection, requiring courage to unmask and face imperfections.

But it's not enough to merely recognize these; one must understand the depth and the influence these weaknesses exert over our lives. It's crucial also to comprehend how these weaknesses manifest themselves, how they affect our behavior, and what triggers them.

4.2. Acknowledging Weaknesses

Once you understand your weaknesses, the next step is acknowledgment. The practice of accepting your flaws without judgment or resistance is transformational. It's not about being hard on yourself or focusing excessively on your shortcomings. Instead, it's about the conscious acceptance of these as part of your current identity.

Acknowledgment is not a passive act; it is a process. It involves engaging with your weakness, analyzing its ramifications, internalizing its existence, and developing a deep-seated resolve to change. It involves recognizing that you have the power to transform and are not doomed to weakness permanently.

4.3. Developing a Strategy to Overcome Weaknesses

A cardinal point to remember is: you're not alone in your journey of overcoming weaknesses. Vulnerabilities are universal; everyone has them, and millions have successfully overcome them.

Creating a detailed, actionable plan is key to conquering your shortcomings. This blueprint should include step-by-step goals, actions, and strategies designed to address your specific weaknesses. Your plan should be outlined with SMART (Specific, Measurable, Achievable, Relevant, Time-bound) goals that give a clear path forward and a way to measure progress.

4.4. Cultivating Patience and Persistence

Overcoming weaknesses is not an overnight process. It demands time, patience, and a great deal of persistence. There will be pitfalls and setbacks, but with perseverance, you'll get there. It's important to prepare for these setbacks and have a strategy to deal with them. Developing resilience, building a support network, and staying motivated despite the pitfalls are crucial aspects of this phase.

4.5. Celebrating Progress

Every step you take towards overcoming your weakness is a victory that deserves celebration. Progress, however small, is still progress. Celebrate your victories, learn from your setbacks, and remember to be kind to yourself along the way. Reflecting on your journey, practicing gratitude, and acknowledging progress can fill you with motivation to continue.

This exhaustive exploration into overcoming weaknesses has guided you through the labyrinthine process of understanding, acknowledging, and mastering your shortcomings. It's a compelling journey of introspection, acceptance, strategic planning, persistence, and celebration. So, dear reader, embrace this process and march forth with conviction and courage. This path, while arduous, leads to extraordinary personal growth, pushing you closer to the peak of your potential. Remember, the strength to overcome your weaknesses lies within you. It is waiting to be discovered, harnessed, and honed to your benefit.

Chapter 5. Building Resilience: The Key to Persistence

Resilience is not merely a trait that we are born with but a skill that can be honed and cultivated. It is the fortitude that empowers us to rise again from the ashes of our failures and to continue unflinchingly on our path to success.

5.1. Understanding Resilience

The first step to building resilience is to understand what it constitutes. Resilience is the ability to withstand adversity and bounce back from difficult life events. It's about being flexible and adaptable in the face of challenges, trauma, tragedy or extreme stress. It is the 'grit' that allows a person to keep pushing on, no matter how arduous their journey becomes.

5.2. The Importance of Resilience

In our chaotic and unpredictable world, resilience is our most formidable ally. It shields us from the curveballs life throws, enabling us to navigate the darkest storms and come out on the other side stronger and wiser. It values the journey as much as the destination, ensuring we learn from the challenges faced, rather than succumb to them. Without resilience, personal growth cannot occur, as it is personal growth that often comes from adversity and hardship.

5.3. Building Blocks of Resilience

While some people come into the world with a higher threshold of resilience than others, it's important to know that resilience can also be built and strengthened over time. Like a muscle, the more we use it, the stronger it becomes.

Life experiences, self-knowledge, relationships and healthy coping mechanisms are among the many building blocks of resilience.

5.4. Building Resilience Through Life Experiences

Life experiences, both good and bad, play a crucial role in building resilience. Every challenge we face and overcome strengthens our resilience muscle and teaches us that we're capable of handling adversity. It's important to remember that no life experience is wasteful. Each event, each experience, is an opportunity to grow and become more resilient.

5.5. Building Resilience Through Relationships

Our relationships significantly influence our resilience. The kind and understanding people in our lives often create a safety net that catches us when we fall. Having strong, supportive relationships helps us to build a positive outlook and a robust resilience.

5.6. Building Resilience Through Healthy Coping Mechanisms

Healthy coping mechanisms are an integral part of building resilience. Instead of turning to harmful habits when faced with stress or adversity, cultivate ways of coping that build resilience and enhance overall well-being. These might include mindfulness, physical activity, adequate sleep, a balanced diet, and seeking professional help when necessary.

5.7. The Role of Persistence in Resilience

Persistence is inexorably linked to resilience. It demands unwavering commitment and an immovable desire to succeed despite the adversity faced. It is about having the mental tenacity to keep going, no matter the obstacles. Over time, persistence can transform the heaviest stones into the smoothest pebbles, turning stumbling blocks into stepping stones on the journey to success.

Just like resilience, persistence is nuanced and multifaceted, entwined with our worldview, our ability to handle stress, adapt to change, and trust in our journey. Building up resilience, therefore, naturally leads to increased persistence, creating an inner resource that drives us to strive harder, reach higher, and never give up.

5.8. A Note on Self-Compassion and Resilience

One crucial element that's often overlooked when discussing resilience is self-compassion. Resilience is not about denying or suppressing emotions in the face of adversity. On the contrary, it's about acknowledging these emotions and allowing oneself the space to feel, to understand, to heal. Self-compassion during difficult times promotes resilience, as it allows us to accept our failures, learn from them, and continue moving forward.

Let's remember: resilience is not a destination but a lifelong journey. Building it calls for patience, persistence, self-belief, and enduring faith in one's abilities. Keep pressing on, my dear reader. Remember, every step forward, every moment of courage, every time you pick yourself up after a fall, you're building resilience. You're forging a fortress of determination and resolve from which you'll conquer legions of challenges and stand triumphant on the battlefield of life.

Cherish your journey and remember - resilience may be the key to persistence, but it's also the key to extraordinary personal growth.

Chapter 6. Mastering Personal Relationships: Nurturing Your Support Network

In today's hyperconnected world, the importance of personal relationships cannot be underestimated. A strong, nurturing, support network is vital not only for emotional wealth but also for a holistic sense of well-being. It is the luscious life-forest we are nestled within, our oasis in the arid desert of stress, and a gust of invigorating fresh breeze in the stifling monotony. Purposefully nurturing these invaluable bonds, therefore, merits our utmost attention.

6.1. The Intricate Webs of Connection

Let's begin by delving into the core fabric of personal relationships — the intricate webs of connection that we, as individuals, create with those around us. This includes relationships with family, friends, mentors, coworkers, and even acquaintances. We all have a network of intricate webs of connection, and each relational strand in this web carries unique resonance.

Your family potentially serves as the basic threadwork for emotional, financial, and social support, sustaining us in times of need and celebrating with us in times of joy. Friends who are outside the purview of our blood bond hold an equally invaluable place in our life mosaic, offering perspectives that inspire growth, challenging us, and being reservoirs of camaraderie and care.

Mentors, on the other hand, are our lighthouses in the storms of uncertainty, their years of wisdom illuminating the smoothest possible path for our journey. Colleagues and coworkers can help us navigate professional hurdles, share knowledge, and provide support during high-pressure situations. Lastly, the wide-spectrum acquaintances across our social circles can often deliver the most unexpected and enriching experiences, escorting our growth in unpredictable ways.

6.2. Nurture, Not Nature: An Active Equation

The beauty of personal relationships lies in the fact that they are not strictly determined by the laws of genetic network - they are open to evolution, growth, and most importantly, nurturing. The notion that relationships just 'happen' is rather passive. We must actively foster these relationships, nurture these bonds, and ultimately create an effective support network that is not merely existent, but also functional and rewarding.

Nurturing may seem daunting – how does one care, feed, and cultivate the countless connections that comprise personal relationships? While it is true that every relationship is unique and might need a distinct nurturing approach, some principles hold almost universally. These include open communication, mutual respect, trust, compromise, and spending quality time together. These principles serve as the lifeblood that continuously circulates within the veins of these intricate webs of connection, fortifying and fueling them.

6.3. The Confluence of Mutual Respect and Trust

Mutual respect and trust often act as twin cornerstones in the solid framework of personal relationships. A relationship devoid of respect is like a ship without a compass, drifting aimlessly at the mercy of the waves. Trust, in its quintessence, is similar to the sturdy anchor that maintains the ship's position in the turbulent sea, preventing it from being swept away.

Hence, investing time and effort in fostering mutual respect and trust is truly invaluable. It requires consistent demonstration of dependability, integrity, and fairness. Although this might seem hefty, the yield of such investments is bountiful and long-lasting.

6.4. Quality Time: The Essential Nourishment

The nutrient-rich humus that catalyzes the thriving of personal relationships is quality time. Merely spending time with those in our network might not prove effective if that time lacks depth and thoughtful engagement. Quality time breathes life into relations, transforming casual connections into strong, dependable bonds.

Whether it's a heartfelt conversation over dinner, a long walk in the park sharing thoughts, heartfelt summertime family trips, or a thoughtful gift that shows how much you care and understand one another, each displays a level of commitment and respect for the relationship that nurtures bonds.

6.5. In Conclusion: A Constant Endeavor

In the end, nurturing personal relationships appears less like a destination and more of an ongoing journey. A journey that potentially entails challenges and upheavals but promises the richness of love, support, and companionship. Nurturing our personal relationships and support network is therefore not a task to be checked off a list; it's a way of life, to be learned, adapted, and implemented as a constant endeavor. By doing so, we ensure our own well-being and precipitate an incremental ripple effect of positivity within our community, taking each other a step closer to extraordinary.

Chapter 7. The Power of Mindfulness: Being Present in the Now

Mindfulness is not a concept conjured from thin air but is deeply rooted in centuries-old philosophies and practices, primarily Buddhism. It is a timeless and universal human capacity, often characterized by a present-oriented awareness, non-judgmental and accepting mindset, and open curiosity towards one's moment-to-moment experience.

7.1. The Essence of Mindfulness

Remember to envision mindfulness as a lens through which you view your universe, a lens that merely observes and does not judge. This particular lens permits you to see every detail, every color, every shape, and every shade, allowing you to experience the world in its most authentic form. Mindfulness is not just about hushing a busy mind or for relaxation alone. Instead, it is the act of being full present to our experiences, thoughts, feelings, and actions without getting attached or overly reactive to them.

7.2. Why is Mindfulness Essential?

In our chaotic lives, the mind constantly shifts between the past and the future, carrying burdens of regret, guilt and fear that erode our present contentment. Mindfulness helps tether our mind to the present moment, providing an anchor to our fleeting thoughts. It aids in reducing stress, improving focus, augmenting resilience, and enhancing mental well-being, to name a few benefits.

7.3. Techniques of Practicing Mindfulness

Mindfulness practices can be meditative, involving focusing on the breath, body sensation, or the silent repetition of a word or phrase. It could also be non-meditative, like mindful walking, eating, or simply doing everyday tasks with full awareness. These practices tune the mind and body into a tranquil state of balanced awareness.

7.4. Tips for Building Mindful Habits

1. Start Small: For beginners, try to incorporate five minutes of mindfulness meditation each day and gradually increase this duration over time.

2. Use Technology: There are numerous mobile applications and online tools that provide guided mindfulness practices.

3. Create a Mindful Environment: Maintain an environment helpful for mindful practice, largely quiet and serene.

4. Practice Regularly: Try to incorporate mindfulness into your daily routine for better outcomes.

5. Be Patient: Mindfulness is not a goal to be achieved, but a journey to be experienced. It is important not to rush but walk this path at your own pace.

7.5. Challenges in Cultivating Mindfulness

Practicing mindfulness may not be a walk in the park. Encountering difficulties such as lack of time, distractions, physical discomfort, or overactive mind can make mindfulness seem like climbing a steep hill at first. It is crucial not to judge ourselves harshly and understand these barriers as natural responses on the way to building this new habit.

7.6. The Impact of Mindfulness: Being Present in the Now

Regular engagement in mindfulness practices can enrich life quality. It can foster self-awareness, improve emotional intelligence, boost concentration, and foster an overall sense of wellbeing. Every activity we conduct mindfully, from the mundane to the special, helps us truly cherish the present moment, infusing our lives with greater joy, satisfaction, and a sense of fulfillment. This report echoes the words of Thich Nhat Hanh, "Life is available only in the present moment".

To dive deep into the power of mindfulness and its benefits, it is essential to remember that it is a lifelong journey. Like learning an instrument, it starts with halting attempts, progress through consistent practice, and eventually turned into a harmonious symphony over time. Begin this journey with an open heart and mind, and enjoy the transformation it brings. Nothing is more precious than being in the present moment. Fully alive, fully aware.

Chapter 8. Everyday Habits Linked to Success: Small Steps, Big Change

Let's start this fulsome exploration by acknowledging a timeless wisdom; success is not achieved through monumental efforts made periodically. Instead, it's the everyday habits—the quiet, often under-recognized, consistent actions that we imbue into our daily lives—which lay a robust foundation for long-lasting success and catalyze profound change. This chapter uncovers this vital key to attaining extraordinary personal growth, taking you through a comprehensive tour of crucial habits linked intimately to success.

8.1. Strong Morning Routines

Mornings wield the power to make or break your day. Aligning your waking hours with positive habits primes your mind for success, setting an optimistic and productive tone that may well persist through the day.

Successful people from history, be it Benjamin Franklin or Maya Angelou, to modern-day heroes like Oprah Winfrey or Elon Musk, they all uphold strong morning routines. Though different in their approaches, they all share a common thread; starting each day on a high note of positivity, productivity, and purpose.

8.2. Regular Exercise

The merits of regular exercise extend beyond physical health. It's a natural mood booster, releasing endorphins that help decrease stress, increase happiness and enhance concentration. As a non-negotiable part of many successful people's routine, regular exercise fosters discipline- reinforcing consistency and commitment, traits obviously linked with success.

8.3. Embracing Lifelong Learning

In our ever-changing world, a commitment to continuous learning is imperative. The capacity to learn, unlearn, and relearn has been hailed by thinkers like Alvin Toffler as the new literacy. Successful people habitually seek to gain knowledge and deepen their understanding, whether by reading, attending courses, or seeking mentors. Likewise, acknowledging that mistakes are part of the learning curve forms an essential facet of this mindset.

8.4. Healthy Eating Habits

Fueling your body with healthful, nutrient-rich foods has a tangible impact on your mental clarity, energy levels, and overall well-being. Habits like skipping meals, eating fast food, or late-night snacking can lead to energy crashes and decreased productivity. Successful people understand the profound connection between mind and body and consistently make choices promoting their physical health.

8.5. The Power of Positive Thinking

The influence of your mind on your reality can't be overstated. Positive thinking does not wave away problems, but it equips you with the confidence, resilience, and optimism needed to tackle them effectively. The everyday habit of maintaining positive thoughts, coupled with self-belief and affirmative speech, is a powerful motivator that propels many successful persons to surpass their goals.

8.6. Time Management

Every individual, from the busiest CEO to the humblest village farmer, has the same 24 hours in a day. Time, thus, is the great equalizer, but how we use it significantly defines our levels of success. Implementing habits like setting SMART (Specific, Measurable, Achievable, Relevant, Time-bound) goals, prioritizing tasks, and avoiding procrastination ensure that you consistently use your time wisely.

8.7. Cultivating Gratitude

Gratitude, though seemingly simplistic, opens up a world of positivity. It fosters the reassurance of abundance, joy, and contentment. Acknowledging your blessings regularly allows you to focus on the good in your life, encouraging a habit of positivity that acts as a cornerstone of success.

As we close this richly detailed discourse, remember this: implementing productive habits is akin to dropping a pebble into a pond. The initial splash embodies the first small change, the ripple effects symbolize the far-reaching transformations these habits are capable of generating in your life. Because, indeed, small steps do lead to big change bounding towards the extraordinary. Changes begin subtly, gently nudging you closer each day to achieving your highest potential, illuminating your path with the brilliance of steady progress towards a more vibrant, successful, and fulfilled version of you. As Lao Tzu wisely stated, "The journey of a thousand miles begins with a single step".

Chapter 9. Motivation is a Muscle: How to Flex It

Just as the body's physical muscles require a regime of regular workouts, discipline, dedication, and a nutrient-rich diet, motivation, metaphorically our mental muscle, calls for the same rigorous approach to be constantly kept at its full strength. Your mind, much like your physical self, can also be trained and toned to its optimal levels to support your engagement with the world around you. It is vital that we acknowledge that motivation is not a static state but is dynamic and perpetually responsive to our actions and attitudes.

9.1. Understanding Motivation: The Animated Force

Motivation is spectacularly fueled by a myriad of factors, and defining it in broad terms allows us to effectively grasp what propels us into action. Essentially, motivation is the internal or external stimulus that compels us to act, behave, or engage in a certain way. This driving force represents a psychological process that catalyzes goal-oriented actions. While the stimuli of motivation could be complex and interrelated, they can generally be classified as intrinsic (inner) motivators that arise from personal enjoyment or interest and extrinsic (outer) motivators influenced by external rewards or penalties.

9.2. Pumping Your Motivational Muscle: Strategies and Techniques

Regular training is crucial in flexing and strengthening your motivational muscle. This section presents several strategic approaches and disciplines that form the essential elements of a regimen of "mental calisthenics".

1. **Setting SMART Goals**: The acronym stands for goals that are Specific, Measurable, Achievable, Relevant, and Time-bound. Clearly defined goals guide your decision-making process and provide a sense of direction, acting as a powerful impetus for motivation.

2. **Creating a Positive Environment**: Ward off negativity by fostering a positive mindset and surrounding yourself with optimism. This energizing force can fan the flames of your motivation, helping you to overcome obstacles and stay focused on your path.

3. **Establishing a Routine and Staying Disciplined**: Consistency catalyzes progress. Establishing routines, implementing daily habits, and maintaining discipline can greatly enhance your ability to flex your motivational muscle.

Each of these strategies acts like a vigorous and individually tailored workout routine that you can incorporate into your daily regimen to progressively enhance your motivational efficacy.

9.3. The Power of Habit: Establishing Repetition

Think of the power of habit as your motivation's indispensable workout partner. Habits are inextricably linked with motivation because they dictate our daily behaviors and patterns. Repeated, meaningful actions amplify motivation levels by creating a loop of positive reinforcement. Formulating a well-structured routine and consciously adhering to it invites success on the path to flexing your motivational muscle.

9.4. Nurturing Emotional Resilience: The Stamina of Motivation

Just as the body is tested by the rigors of physical exercise, motivation also encounters challenges. Therefore, it's beneficial to foster resilience to confront disappointments or potential setbacks. Emotional resilience equips you with the mental strength required for confronting failures and transforming them into stepping stones for growth, thus maintaining motivation in the face of adversity.

9.5. Conclusion: A Tireless March

Certainly, motivation functions much like a muscle. It requires consistent activation and exertion to keep it robust and ready for action. By embracing and incorporating the recommended calisthenics of mind into your routine, you can flex and expand this essential muscle, charting your path to an extraordinary journey of ongoing personal growth and achievement. Remember, like any workout plan, it's imperative to track progress, celebrate victories, and readjust strategies according to the ebb and flow of motivation. Start today, for the path to the extraordinary begins with a single step fueled by the power of motivation.

Chapter 10. Fostering Creativity and Curiosity: The Lifelong Learner's Toolkit

One of the cornerstones of reaching our fullest potential often lies in fostering creativity and curiosity, especially with a focus for lifelong learning. The ability to maintain curiosity, to constantly learn, and to leverage that knowledge in innovative, creative ways, is truly a potent tool in your journey towards personal growth. This chapter delves into strategies and techniques that will empower you to become a lifelong learner, a fountainhead of creativity, and a wellspring of curiosity.

10.1. Familiarize with the Concept of Lifelong Learning

Learning is an unending journey that stretches beyond school years, beyond obtaining degrees, and reaches into every single moment of our lives. Lifelong learning is steeped in the pursuit of knowledge for personal or professional reasons. It enhances our understanding of the world around us, furnishing us with more and better opportunities and enriching our lives.

In essence, a lifelong learner is someone who is committed to the perennial pursuit of knowledge and growth. These individuals are inherently curious, open-minded, and always willing to learn new skills, whether it's out of necessity, interest, or the simple joy of learning itself. Lifelong learners know that every experience – good or bad – provides a learning opportunity.

10.2. Cultivating a Curious Mindset

Curiosity, that ever-present, innate, childlike quality is something that can be pushed to the fringes as we age and face the pressing concerns of adult life. Yet, it is curiosity, an insatiable quest for knowledge, that fuels our desire to understand, innovate, and improve.

Cultivating a curious mindset requires that we remain receptive to new ideas and open the doors of our minds to diverse thoughts, opinions, and experiences. Biases, preconceived notions, and rigid beliefs often serve as roadblocks on this path. By cultivating an attitude of openness, by asking questions, and by developing a healthy skepticism that challenges the status quo, we can truly nurture our curiosity.

10.3. Nurturing Creativity

Creativity, like curiosity, can often be suppressed under the weight of everyday responsibilities. However, creativity is not confined to the arts. It is our ability to think beyond the conventional, to connect the seemingly unconnected, and to birth ideas that bring about change and innovation.

Creativity thrives in an environment of freedom – freedom to think, to dream and to make mistakes. It's important to build this environment for ourselves, giving ourselves permission to be creative, taking risks, and venturing into the unknown. Regularly setting aside time for creative pursuits, whether they are directly related to your work or not, can help you adapt better to unexpected situations, find ingenious ways to overcome challenges, and constantly innovate in all aspects of your life.

10.4. The Art of Balancing Curiosity and Creativity

Curiosity and creativity, though mutually exclusive, are profoundly interconnected. The best way to envision this connection might be as a cycle: starting with curiosity, spiraling into exploration, culminating in creativity, and then beginning anew. The art lies in balancing these two forces and understanding that each feeds the other.

Exploratory behavior, fueled by curiosity, can lead to broader thinking and the generation of fresh ideas, which is the very essence of creativity. It is important to invest time to nurture both – they are two sides of the same coin – essential weapons in your arsenal on the journey towards personal growth.

10.5. Tools and Techniques to Foster Curiosity and Creativity

Now that we have firmly established the WHY of curiosity and creativity let's delve into some concrete tools and techniques to foster these essential qualities.

- Read Widely and Diversely: Encourage curiosity by immersing yourself in a variety of sources, disciplines, and viewpoints. This helps broaden your knowledge base and expose you to a range of different perspectives and ideas.

- Cultivate Openness: Adopt an open attitude where feedback is welcomed, mistakes are seen as learning opportunities, and new ideas are enthusiastically explored.

- Practice Mindfulness: By paying attention to our thoughts and feelings without judgment, we can develop a richer appreciation of our experiences, fostering creativity in the process.

- Embrace Uncertainty: Be comfortable with ambiguity and uncertainty. It is often in these spaces that creativity is sparked and innovative ideas are born.

- Engage in Reflection: Regularly set aside time to reflect on your learning and experiences. This practice can enhance both self-understanding and problem-solving skills, thereby boosting creativity.

To close this chapter, it is important to remember that curiosity sparks the desire to learn and explore, while creativity is the ability to transform those discoveries into something original and valuable. By fostering these qualities and continually learning, you can build a lifetime toolkit that allows for adaptation, resilience, and dynamic personal growth.

Chapter 11. Celebrating Progress: The Power of Gratitude and Reflection

Our own personal voyage towards growth and fulfillment is punctuated with milestones—small victories and transformative breakthroughs that, while often incredibly rewarding in their own right, serve a secondary and equally critical function. They stand as potent reminders of our path, our journey, our progress.

11.1. The Importance of Celebrating Progress

In many instances, the incessant pursuit of growth and personal betterment may inadvertently render us myopic, blurring our vision from recognizing the fruit of our efforts, the manifestation of our labor. Caught up in the continual aspiration of reaching out for more, we may overlook the ground we've already covered, the mountains we've already scaled.

Celebrating progress is an act as therapeutic as it is revelatory. It allows us one of life's fundamental joys—to pause, survey the landscape of our accomplishments, and feel a sense of pride and satisfaction. More so, it serves as a springboard, amplifying our drive for further growth. We inherently crave validation and a sense of achievement. Failing to acknowledge and celebrate our progress can result in feelings of inadequacy and stagnation.

Appreciating your progress fuels your journey towards self-growth. It fosters an environment of self-love, celebrates your effort, strengthens your motivation, and amplifies your self-esteem. It defines your progress not by the distance left to travel but by the ground already covered.

11.2. The Role of Gratitude in Growing

Parallel to the act of celebrating progress runs the art of gratitude. Gratitude, at its core, is a profound emotional state of acknowledging the gifts and the advantages life has bestowed upon us. It is a sense of thanksgiving and appreciation for what we have, as opposed to a focus on what we lack. The art of gratitude is, in essence, a practice that encourages positive thinking by forcing us to shift our mental focus from the negatives and uncertainties of life to the positives and certainties.

Studies reveal that regular practice of gratitude can lead to feelings of increased well-being, reduced depression and anxiety, improved sleep, and a generally more optimistic outlook on life. This is because gratitude stimulates the brain's hypothalamus, which manages stress, and the ventral tegmental area, part of our brain's reward system. Expressing gratitude initiates a virtuous cycle in our brains, releasing dopamine and serotonin—the neurotransmitters responsible for feelings of contentment.

In the context of personal growth, gratitude lays the fertile ground for the seeds of progress to thrive. It conditions us to seek the silver lining in every cloud, to draw learning from each setback, and to find joy in every triumph, no matter how small.

11.3. The Power of Reflective Practice

Reflection is a systematic methodology for personal improvement. As defined by Donald Schön in his book "The Reflective Practitioner," reflection is a conversation with oneself about experiences, learning, and understanding. It's a profound practice that allows us to unearth lessons hidden in our experiences, to formulate strategies based on our past, and to paint a broader, clearer picture of our journey.

Reflection provides an insightful retrospective view of our journey; it aids in anchoring the significance of our fleeting experiences and emotions, thereby collecting the wisdom they carry. Reflecting on our journey—in our struggles and triumphs—not only facilitates the consolidation of our experiences and the lessons they entail, but also allows us to gain an appreciation for our journey and the way it shaped us.

11.4. Integrating Celebrations, Gratitude, and Reflection into Daily Life

Begin by carving out a sacrosanct time slot each day exclusively dedicated to your reflective practice, gratitude, and celebration. This could be during the early hours of the morning, setting a positive, appreciative tone for the day ahead, or during the quieter hours of the night, closing the day on a note of reflection and gratitude.

Next, acquire a gratitude journal. This will serve as a recorded manifesto of your journey. Each day, jot down the wins of the day, no matter how small. Celebrate these wins, revel in the feeling of accomplishment. This simple act of recognition and celebration will enhance your motivation, boost your confidence, and fuel your growth process.

Then, cultivate the habit of gratitude. Note down daily aspects you feel grateful for. They could be as grand as a job promotion or as simple as a morning coffee. The size of the act doesn't matter; the grace lies in acknowledging it. Cultivating this will enable a shift towards positive thinking and foster a conducive environment for growth.

Finally, indulge in a daily reflective practice. Review your experiences, interactions, and emotions for the day. Seek patterns, identify lessons, and apply these to upcoming endeavors. By consciously introspecting, you make your experiences a wellspring of growth-inducing wisdom.

In conclusion, celebrating progress, expressing gratitude, and practicing reflection might seem like simple practices, yet they are profoundly transformative. Studiously applying these can serve as powerful catalysts for personal growth, guiding you gradually yet assuredly to the extraordinary summit of personal achievement and fulfillment.

www.ingramcontent.com/pod-product-compliance
Lightning Source LLC
Chambersburg PA
CBHW060901260726
48661CB00008B/3378